P♡etry

Zoe Phillips

Published by New Generation Publishing in 2019

First Edition

www.newgeneration-publishing.com

To mummy and daddy

I miss you both

Whatever the weather
Whatever the day
I’ll love you in each and every way

Can’t you hear my tears?

Babe, darling,
Can’t you hear my tears
Something’s starting
Can’t you feel my fears
If there’s any more to say
I beg you, hold me one more day

I turn around and see your face
I face the ground, to feel your embrace
For every pebble I can see
It just means the whole world to me
        Is watching us,
        Waiting for us
        Making, anticipating us

Your every move just turns my eye
You’re there to prove you’re just another guy
But in my heart, I hold a place for you
In my soul, I love you through and through

You ‘phoned last night
To say ‘Hello’
‘I love you girl’ or innuendo

Is your heart as cold as ice
Surely you're not one sacrifice?
'I love you' or is that a word
That in your mind sounds too absurd

Got so many things to say

I've got so many things to say
But I just can't find the words.
I've a list of things to do
But they all seem too absurd.
For if you could see into my eyes
(I'm searching for the light)
I'm falling to my destiny
I've just gotta fight.

When I reach out my hand
Will you be there?
When I talk about my world
Will you sit and stare?
Or will you listen to me
I've some things I've gotta say
If you could understand my love
I'm sure you'd want to stay

If you call me on the 'phone
I just can't hang the line
Despite the hateful calls you make
I just can't break my mind
I just can't seem to hesitate
To pause, or to abstain
Oh can't you see, I'm foolishly

In love with you again

When you say that you're a user
Does that just mean to say
You're a glutton for your one night stands
And I'm one night you can't explain?
Oh tell me if you're using me
For I can't stand the pain
Break us before I break my heart
Though it's cracking all the same

Got so many things to say
I just can't find the words
I've a list of things to do
But they all seem too absurd
Oh if you could see into my eyes
If you could taste my tears
I've fallen to my destiny
Oh help me don't just leave me here
I love you or is that a phrase
Which in your mind, does not appear

Breaking, oh I'm breaking up above your love
Shaking, oh I'm shaking 'til I never will be stirred

Oh never will be never
When you're ever
In my mind
So hold me close and let's make up
Or else just let me hear the truth –
Whatever will, it never will
Whoever or whenever 'til
You just can't see
You just wont see
I just to face the fact you will
Never be my love again

I thought we had something in this
When one night we had so much bliss
But next day was square one again
Who'd have believed that we had kissed
With so much ecstasy
That you'd admitted your three woes
You loved me, or is that your destiny?
I answered in a similar way
But wasn't that enough?
You'll never be dam happy, but you'll
never be downcast
They'll be victims just like me
Who'll fall into you're trap

Oh I’m breaking up, I’m breaking down
I’m breaking through your love

I’ve so many things to say
But I just can’t find the words
I’ve a list of things to do
But they all seem too absurd
So I’ll sing this song for you to hear
If you can’t hear my tears
Oh I’ll sing aloud, sing to the crowds –
My destiny it must be near

I’ve sold my heart to you alone
I see there’s no way of getting it back
again

Why?

Why?
Did I bother to ring
Why?
Do I try hard to sing
Why?
There's an answer somewhere
Why?
Does it mean you just don't care

All day
I wait to say 'hello'
All night
I long to see you
When then
Will you return my call
'Til then
am I just your fool

Last night
What happened to you?
'When?'
when I tried to get through
Out?
'yeah, just having a laugh'
I see

Just don’t bother telling me
To spare me the pain
I love you too much to
Let it happen again

Why?
Do I bother to ring
Why?
Do I try hard to sing
Why?
Must be an answer someplace
Why?
I can see it in your face

Believe me, too

I'm drinking the strongest coffee I can find
and sit in the softest chair
To think of you, it breaks my mind
I can only sit and stare

I never meant you to take it that way
If only you understood
Whenever I see you, my heart breaks away
When I say I love you,
I mean it forever
And not just for today

A car drives up outside, as I begin to stand
I strain my eyes to look for you
But I should know you'll never come around
When I said I was sorry
I meant it forever
And not just for yesterday

I used to pray for all my worth
To look as cool as you
But if God won't grant my wishes

What should I do?
Will it mean you'll pass me by
Without a nod or grin?
But I'll remember how we used to be

"perfect'
Heaven wasn't the word – we had
misunderstandings
But all in all we know it was love
Too young?
Or was it just we did not understand
Each and other?

And now, as I sip my last dreg
A lump forms in my throat
The 'phone rings and I pick it up –
will you just hang the line?
No – sorry echoes through my head
And I believe you
Yes, believe me too

Pink Cloud

There's a pink cloud
Hanging above my head –
And what it sends
Is not just rain
But hope in a shade of blue

Oh blue
So new and white
So you
Oh hold your head up high you say
Or you're just deigned to die, you say

Come rain, come shine
I'll keep my pink cloud
Above my head
To shower its spectrum on me
When I'm in bed
And I think of you

Oh blue
So new and white
So you
Oh hold your head up high you say
Or you're just deigned to die you say

One day, my cloud,
It'll fly away
And with it, memories will fly too
In a paler shade of blue

Wait, the sun's come out
It's broken up the sky –
It's broken up my mind
But I still find it hard
Not to be reminded
Of you

Pink cloud, don't leave me
Cold and bare
Pink cloud, stay by me
Tell me if he cares
Pink cloud
Oh pink cloud
So blue

(Oh why so blue,
Pink cloud, why blue – oh blue)
Believe me

Please believe me –
I accept your apology
And so if we're to see each other again –

Will we fall in love
Or will we just stop and stare

Please believe me –
I'm sorry too
I hope that now we can understand
Each other

Please believe me –
I know your hi-fi life
Don't pretend I know nothing of
your excuses
To be without me

Please believe me –
I have my flings
So now we're matched, so let's be straight
And start from dot again

I'm sorry too
I hope that now we understand
When love is due

One heart together, now

They tell me miracles don't happen very
soon
I'm glad to see we're one exception to that
rule
For when I first set eyes on you
And when you first set eyes on me
And now our love together – let us be – let
us be

One heart together now
So happy
So happy that forever we're to start
Our feelings, one everlasting art

They tell me pardise is very hard to find
Well now that you're with me, they'll
have to change their minds
It's just you lay me down –
I find it hard to frown
We hold the future ever in our arms – let
us be – oh let us be

One destiny together
Ever happy
That forever we're to start

Our feelings – one everlasting art

They've warned me of my gift of love before,
That special feeling comes upon me more and more
When you're with me
One heart together now
So happy
So happy that forever we're to start
Our feelings, one everlasting art
One destiny together
Ever happy
That forever we're to start
Our feelings – one everlasting art

Tiger light

The snake bite rattles
In the paupers grave
And my world lies lost
I'm gone
I tremble
Liar – how could you
See through my skin
Through the jungle here
My mind's not so clear
Tell me –
Is it new
Tell me
What is truth

Trust is one big word
My mamma used to say
But now, I stare in disbelief
Tiger light
Shining
Oh so bright
Blinding
Loves first sight
Across the dance floor

I hear a car roll up outside
I wait for a knock
And all I hear
Are footsteps
As they walk away

Well you've been dragging me along
I think it's time for me
To make you see
You're not
The only fish in the sea

Passion hiss
In the silent kiss
Of moonlight
Loving tomb
Open – all my gloom
Is scattered in your ash
Tiger light
Shining
Oh so bright
Blinding
Love's first sight
Across the dancefloor

Come rain, fall
Fall victim to the flood
Just like my brotherhood
Shed your tears
Come lightening fire
Streak your limits with me the glow
To me, let you show
All your glamour
For I see it in my world tonight
Stars so bright, yet dull
If you could unveil my senses, moon
My glowing doom
Would curse you all.

Open earth, let thunder break
Wild ponies take
Me away
From it all
Galloping shire
Falls victim to the road
With me its heavy load
In the mire
Falling to the mud
Cry your brotherhood
Into the fire

My story's been told
But once forever
My fortune's sold
But will be never
Sold again
My fable's gone
My motto too
It was all in vain
That I 'phoned you
Or that's how it seems
Oh why let us be
One destiny
Together
Never happy
That forever we'll be free
We'll be free
Oh can't you see…

Rain

Each drop of rain
Drives me away
So you can imagine my pain
Now there's a storm

Each drop of rain
Drives me insane
With my memories it falls
'till its puddles become my cause
of it all

some make it through the rain
can we do the same?
Or are we lost in the wind
Don't remind me, do something
To avoid
My all

My all is hate – it must be,
Or you'd ask me to stay
My all is fate that is real
I was destined to be
Born –
Into the rain

Drive it away – or drive me
Your option must be hasty
Don’t rebuke
Don’t waste time
Just tell me why
Then hang the line

The prayer

When the time is right
I'll say yes
I see you've put your trust in me
In you, I'll do the same
But I'll take time
That's how it's done
You should accept my point of view
If you understand and knew

Yes I do feel the same
It's just tonight it's not the name
I said next week
But I should have known
I've read in your horoscope
How you disown, your patience
In my mind

Please God
Please let him wait for me
Please God
Oh can't you make him see
Please God
I've been a fool all along
Don't try telling me now.
Because I know I've been wrong

I’ve been wrong to my soul
I’ve decided, even me
But now
Now that I understand
Please God take my problem
Into your hand

Tell me if he’s my destiny

Anyone who's anyone

Last night I had to ring
To say I'm sorry, say I'm sorry
It was my last highland fling
But you don't worry, you won't worry
Hello, how are you?
Hey, what's your game?
Will you do things my way
Or maybe we should talk about it

Well, you were out again
I don't need you, I don't need you
But I got a strange feeling
From all we've been through, where
we've been to
Let's talk about it
Let's think us through
Will you do things my way
Or maybe we should talk about it

Tonight, you had to 'phone
(To) say 'I love you', say 'I love you'
ok, so I went out
out without you, out without you
Hey look at my heartache
I feel the same

So let's do things my way
Or maybe we should talk about it

I went out last night
Now I've got me a brand new boyfriend
So? Anyone who's anyone is
What they want to be
Now I've got me a brand new boyfriend
Because maybe now is the time to make
you see

Anyone who's, anyone is
Who
…?

Refund my heart

You bought my heart at retail price
It was going cheap just at that time
But only to you
Was it for sale
Only for you
Did I sit on the shelf

I thought I'd get a bargain
Selling my heart for yours
But my hopes were all too gone
When I saw you at the stores
Was her heart as good as mine?
Could it love and beat and chime?
Was it cheap at just that time?

Now refund my heart to me
(I want no money)
Oh, save my heart, then leave me be
Go find your gift and budget tree
'cos I'm not hangin' around
whilst you're foolin' and flappin'
I'm bound
For Tahiti

You may be the pick of the bunch

But I couldn't be bothered a punch
Fresh fruits my choice from now on
Nothing sour or bitter
Will turn me on
So hang it all, if you want me
And choose your crops with ecstasy
For if I'm choice
I'll be your fool again
And if I'm not
I'll have my refund all the same

Whatever I may

Faces shine
Then turn away
To show another smile
Truth nods
Then turns to lie
There ends my golden mile

Then should I try
Keep my face straight
Or forever close my mouth
For now, I'm thinking
I don't know
Whatever I say
I'm not sure

Whatever I may
I'm being told
Get your head out of the clouds

I turn
To face another page
Another rainy day
If these clouds were all gone
I'm sure I'd wanna stay
I don't know

Which way I'm heading
My mind's confused
Your love, I'll be sending
Away…

Whatever I may
I'm being told
Get your head out of the clouds

So now I'm on the road
No reaching your path again
Don't try to save me
Don't try to understand
All I want is for me
To get my head out of the clouds

On the run
Out
Of the rain
Free
I need this time (too considerate)
To save my head from the clouds

Idle gossip

I am so unsure
I don't know what to believe
For I've heard so many things
What would you do
If you heard the same
What would you do
In my shoes?

The guitar man
He sings and struts
And the words he says are
All the words
I've been trying to put together
For so long

Love is not demanding
So I've heard it say
It can't be us who've got it wrong
Or perhaps we may
Where's your suggestion?
Where's your complaint?
Or is it idle gossip, caught in play?

One moment in time
I feel as high as the moon

When you're with me
The next, you tear me down –
Don't you expect me to frown?
Surely you understand
What hurts

Love is not demanding
So I've heard it say
It can't be us who've got it wrong
Or perhaps we may
Am I your suggestion?
Am I your complaint?
Am I idle gossip, when you're caught in
play?

Ditty

Smooth, cool
Sophisticated blue
Neat, sweet
You almost broke my heart
But if I had a
Sapphire life
You small town boy

So many things

So many things
I would have wanted you to know
But it's too late now
They tell me you're back
But I don't want to know
Its all too late, too late now
I can see you
As you bragg the finishing call –
It had ended though before
It's had its fall
It's too late
Much too late
Yeah, it's too late now

You tell me you were jealous
I believe you, then I don't
'Cos reminding me are
All your smiles at them
I remember the days we got on so well
But it's just too late
Much too late now
Perhaps I'm living in the past –
I just wanna forget
'cos it's too late now
I'll forget all those good times

Plus forget the rest
‘cos it’s too late now
You tell me they’ll be knocking
But I don’t want to know
My heart has broken once
Now I’m not letting it go
It’s been too late
Just too late
To know

C’mon I hear you say – it’s been a year
Perhaps a break will make us
Appreciate each other’s near
But as far as I can see
It is just an excuse
‘Cos it’s too late – yeah – too late
and much too late now.
Yeah – pain’s too great – now it’s too late
I just wish you fate, now
Fate now, fate now

Baby don't forget

Baby don't forget
It wasn't me who turned my back and ran
Too good's
Like heaven here –
You saw and took it then.
But now, cry out my name
Too bad – I'm not to blame
Anymore

I see your friend, walk down the street
She smugly smiled at me –
And splashed the water
In my face
Walking across the street

Barren smiles
And sudden cries
Stimulate my sleep
I rest alive until I die
My watch
Your eyes
Will keep

But stay again and walk on by –
Not with me

By your side
Crazed by lies, look and cut
Beauty salon
The razor's edge
And now the world lies waiting
At your door –
Or so you say

The time has come to open wide
Let no-one block your way
I know you'll stand
Without my hand
By your side to guide
I hope you;ll stay
Here one day

My sapphire sky to find -
A jewel in my heart
A gem in eye
A star your path to guide
As crystal dewdrops
Seal my doom.

The player

Was it because you loved her so
That you drove me home last night?
To see her flirt with other guys
Did that hurt your pride?
And now you need someone to hold you
A shoulder to cry on
It's not that I don't love you
It's just I feel used when you feel blue
I'd like to help you when in trouble
I would like to help you when in pain
Please god so let him help me
When I hear her call his name
When I feel blue
Just as blue too

Somehow I feel
I'm just a game
And you're the player
A player casts his hand on deck
And faces up, at his request
He throws away
And then picks up.

I guess he's out to win
To toss the dice

And spin roulette
To cast your eyes one way
And set your aim

You've shot me with the silver bullet
Your love like fire has
Rippled through my heart
And now I die
In fact I cry
Your aim has maimed my pitiless sign
And now you've run, your hand in mine
Just chasing clouds out of line

Golden castles in the air
And sweet birds calling 'you're not there'
And now I'm lost in time and space

Crazy for your love

God only knows how much I love you and
He's the only one who knows that I care
Hear me again
I don't want to lose you
I've lost you once too often – I swear

And now I'm crazy for your love –
Yes, for you
It drives me crazy
When I think –
What we used to do
Heaven knows how much I miss you
When in bed alone. I lie
Oh won't you please forgive me
I'll be yours
And you'll be mine

As time ticks on – another night
Without you by my side
Bring back the love you stole from me
You'll need my hand to find
That someone's crazy for your love
Yes, for you
It drives that someone cray
When they think

What they used to do

Heaven knows how much they miss you
When in bed, alone, they lie
Oh won't you please forgive me
And two hearts
Together bind

I hear footsteps creep outside my door
So I run to look for more
It's a vision of your face I see
I knew it couldn't be true

But someone knows I'm crazy for your love
I'm crazy just for you
It drives me crazy
When I think of what
Together we used to do –
Heaven knows how much I miss you
When in bed alone, I lie
Oh won't you please forgive me –
I'll be yours and you'll be mine
Forever
Oh won't you please forgive me
Now I realize my crime
Heaven's gonna pull us back together

I'll be yours
And you'll be mine
Until the end of time
You'll be mine
I'll be yours
And you'll be mine (forever)
And I'll be yours

Just be good to me

Baby, how do I pull myself to say
That you don't love me anyway
Perhaps it's that time's so difficult
For you

I try to explain how I feel today
But my emotions have been washed away
It's true, to suppose
You don't feel the way I do
About you

You make me feel so lonely
It's crazy but I still love you
Call me up and be 'phoney
That is just what you do

From tonight
my attitude will change
From tonight
I'll say you're not to blame
But you
Can stay the same
And you
Can go, just walk away

What you think you know
Is nothing
What you say, you don’t suppose
Here today, and gone tomorrow
Up the dawn and down she goes

You’re a way
You’re a may
You’re a hey - superstar
And you know
Every girl that you pull
Won’t go far

What you think you know
Is nothing
What you say, you don’t suppose
Here today, and gone tomorrow
Up the dawn and down she goes

You’re away
You’re a may
You’re a hey – superstar
And you know
Every girl that you pull
Won’t go far

And it's me that's time to see
You're a user in the highest degree
And a song
For the girl
Who will see who you are

You're look, I guess
Attracted me
You're personality
Is dam all
Still it seems to be
A tragedy
Infatuation ruled one and all

"People always telling me,
You're a user
I don't care about the other girls
Just be good to me"

Disillusion

When I close my eyes
I dream of signs
My world is spinning by
My heart is split
My mind is flicked
Oh help my disillusion

A clock can chime no tear
Two hands linked in fear
As the tick is gone
My dream's undone
Your world is won
My dream's just an illusion

Disillusion my illusion
If you say you love me too
And cohesion by adhesion
Let our forces be renewed

Is it because you're playing games
My mind begins to ache
And all the while
My arms beguile
Let my illusion be my fate
Put an end to all this heartache

Ignorance will be my goal
Until I want to see your soul
Your heart and mine
Two hands entwined
I can see it now, as you hang the line
The truth is loose
No comfort hidden in time

Disillusion your illusion
When I say I love you too
Add cohesion by adhesion
Let our forces be renewed

Disillusion my illusion
If you say you love me too
Add cohesion by adhesion
Let our forces be renewed
Let our worlds become as one
Let my pain just be undone

I’ve fallen in love with you

I don’t think I’ll ever know
Or ever understand
Don’t think that you could know
You never hold my hand
And now the time has come
The time to sell my heart
It’s not second hand
This love of mine
But it’s pulling us apart

Somehow
There’s somewhere
time and space
A place for us to be
But time to pick up what we lost
Seems like eternity
Feels like the break
Broke off the mark
And now we’re young and free
Oh how I hate to hear the voice
I know is not talking to me

I guess you never knew
How much your love was on my mind
But now I think the time has come

For you to realize
Perhaps too late
I just don’t care
I just want you to know
I never loved no-one as much
Because
I’ve fallen in love with you

"Let's go for a coffee"

Conditioned my tresses
Drew me Cilla Black's dresses

Put rags in my locks to make them curl
And stitches in my ballet skirts to make them swirl

Whisked me 'round Jersey Pottery in the sun
Whilst Daddy and Paula played golf, having fun

Accompanied me to Cambridge to meet the Dons
Staved off boyfriends she thought not the ones

Squeezed the blackheads from my nose
Encouraged me to wear brownie badges, which arose

Checked seams on my outfits to ensure they were perfect
Fighting my corner to help me become prefect

Disappointed I only made deputy head girl
Recalling the order mark for leaving my instrument, in a whirl

Proud of my speech prizes and cups galore
I worked hard to please her like never before

Listening to my play and speak at Alderley Edge festivals
The guitar group "Colours", performances so special

Watching me try the catwalk parade
And a small spark of pride I could tell from her ways

She babysat countless times for the Chinese
Coming home with oodles of lemon chicken and teas
The treats we had at the Yang Sing
Kelly the cat took left overs from her knees

Popped down to London to visit the Queen,

Well, Buckingham Palace, on Elizabeth's opening year
Staying with me in Bucks and Battersea Rise
Taking her for dinner, Phantom and all sorts of surprise

My moving to Switzerland was an awful tear
Unable to get back as much as I cared
But she moved to be close to her 3 grandchilds
A very brave call for a Manchester gal'

Though I don't think in Leicester she did fully unpack
Our short times together were spent shopping for food, slippers and slacks
Of any colour as long as they were red
Rubies, roses and bows for Dougal or big ted

Even without car we managed in strife,
Through navigating bus routes in the old country life
Off we went to Stoney Cove and Narborough Manor

Chiswick House and Althorp, a Downton admirer
How we had great visions for a grand life of glamour

No daddy to go to, she was my rock and my world
In a world full of darkness, I tried to comfort her woes

The hospital stays, they would not defeat us
I stole a wheelchair from Glenfield at one point to treat us
Nothing could stop that shopping connection
And off we would trot to the M&S convention.

Slowly I witnessed a life ever ebbing
And knew our adventures would steadily descend into nothing
It's hard to accept and to understand
Why a life I had hoped for was removed from one's hand
Although you are told any day it could happen

It’s never today or tomorrow or so sudden

If there’s one wish I hope for today of all days
Is that mummy is happy and not suffering in her old ways

She’s free again to dance in that ballroom
To make those fine dresses she drew for me often.

I want to continue her legacy and pride
To ensure that my seams all match at the sides
To ensure that I look my best and most proper
Because you never quite know who you meet in the offing

I hope that she meets up with Uncle Ernie and Grandma
And that one of them now says “Let’s go for a coffee”

Zoe Phillips
In memory of Mummy
11th June 2016

www.ingramcontent.com/pod-product-compliance
Ingram Content Group UK Ltd.
Pitfield, Milton Keynes, MK11 3LW, UK
UKHW041842200726
13854UKWH00005BA/1992
9 781789 554106